ULTIMATE MANGA
HOW TO DRAW
MANGA MECHA

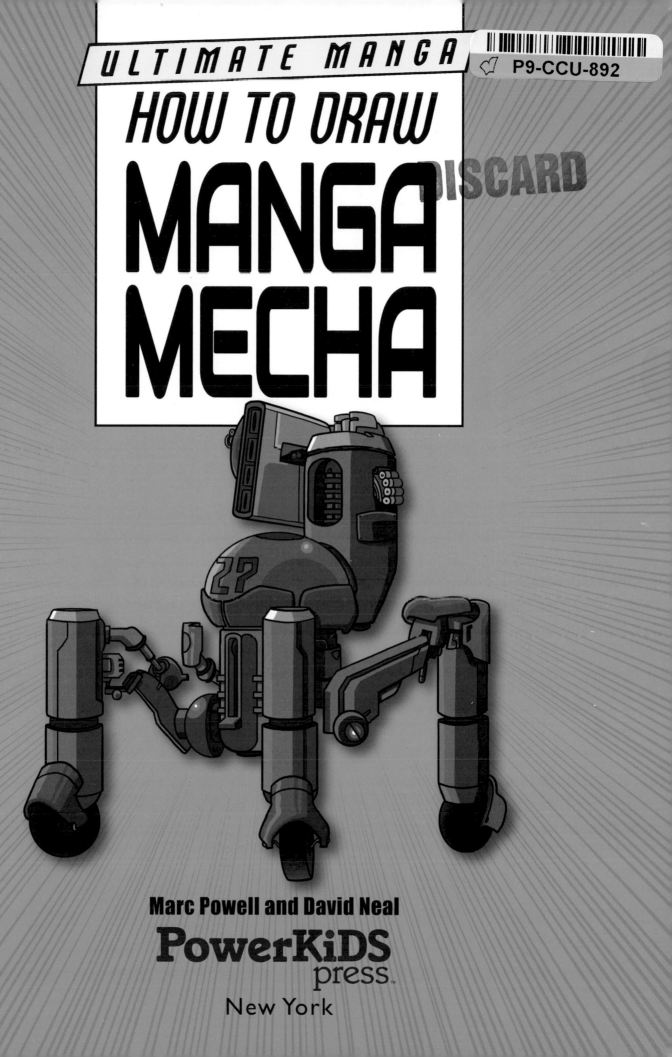

Marc Powell and David Neal

PowerKiDS press

New York

WITH THANKS TO ODA, STEVE, AILIN, AND PAT

Published in 2016 by **The Rosen Publishing Group**
29 East 21st Street, New York, NY 10010

Text by Jack Hawkins
Edited by Jack Hawkins
Designed by Dynamo Ltd and Emma Randall
Cover design by Notion Design
Illustrations by Marc Powell and David Neal

Cataloging-in-Publication Data
Powell, Marc.
How to draw manga mecha / by Marc Powell and David Neal.
p. cm. — (Ultimate manga)
Includes index.
ISBN 978-1-4994-1145-4 (pbk.)
ISBN 978-1-4994-1154-6 (6 pack)
ISBN 978-1-4994-1184-3 (library binding)
1. Comic books, strips, etc. — Japan — Technique — Juvenile literature.
2. Cartooning — Technique — Juvenile literature. 3. Machinery in art —
Juvenile literature. I. Title.
NC1764.5.J3 P694 2016
741.5'1—d23

Manufactured in the United States of America
CPSIA Compliance Information: Batch WS15PK: For Further Information
contact Rosen Publishing, New York, New York at 1-800-237-9932

CONTENTS

HOW TO USE THIS BOOK

The drawings in this book have been built up in seven stages. Each stage uses lines of a different color so you can see the new layer clearly. Of course, you don't have to use different colors in your work. Use a pencil for the first four stages so you can get your drawing right before moving on to the inking and coloring stages.

Stage 1: Green lines
This is the basic stick figure of your character.

Stage 2: Red lines
The next step is to flesh out the simple stick figure.

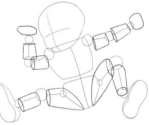

Stage 3: Blue lines
Then finish the basic shape and add in extra details.

Stage 4: Black lines
Add in clothes and any accessories.

Stage 5: Inks
The inking stage will give you a final line drawing.

Stage 6: Colors
"Flat" coloring uses lighter shades to set the base colors of your character.

Stage 7: Shading
Add shadows for light sources, and use darker colors to add depth to your character.

BASIC TOOLS

You don't need lots of complicated, expensive tools for your manga images – many of them are available from a good stationery shop. The others can be found in any art supplies store, or online.

PENCILS

These are probably the most important tool for any artist. It's important to find a type of pencil you are comfortable with, since you will be spending a lot of time using it.

Graphite

You will be accustomed to using graphite pencils – they are the familiar wood-encased "lead" pencils. They are available in a variety of densities from the softest, 9B, right up to the hardest, 9H. Hard pencils last longer and are less likely to smudge on the paper. Most artists use an HB (#2) pencil, which falls in the middle of the density scale.

Mechanical pencils

Also known as propelling pencils, these contain a length of lead that can be replaced. The leads are available in the same densities as graphite pencils. The great advantage of mechanical pencils over graphite is that you never have to sharpen them – you simply extend more lead as it wears down.

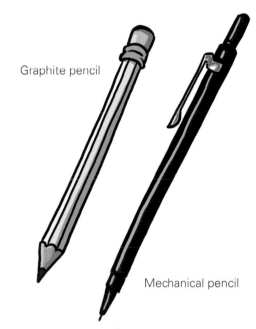

Graphite pencil

Mechanical pencil

INKING PENS

After you have penciled your piece of artwork, you will need to ink the line to give a sharp, solid image.

Ballpoint pens

Standard ballpoint pens are ideal for lining your piece. However, their quality varies, as does their delivery of ink. A single good-quality ballpoint pen is better than a collection of cheap ones.

Marker pens

Standard marker pens of varying thicknesses are ideal for coloring and shading your artworks. They provide a steady, consistent supply of ink, and can be used to build layers of color by re-inking the same area. They are the tools most frequently used for manga coloring.

Marker

Ballpoint pen

ABANDONED ROBOT

In the world of the future there might be some rusty old robots like this, just waiting for their time to be useful again. It's a neat twist to create a mecha that isn't shiny and new but looks like it has had a rough life.

STEP 1
Draw a robot stick figure with high ankle joints leading to wedge-shaped feet.

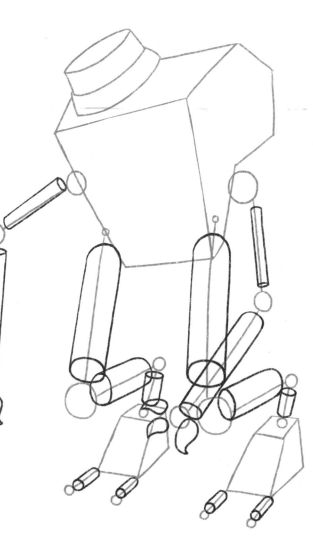

STEP 2
Use cylinder shapes to give bulk to your robot's arms and legs and draw two narrow cylinders extending from each foot. Add three claws at the end of each arm.

STEP 3
Add more parts to your robot, which is made up of a jumble of components.

STEP 4
Draw in the details on the robot's various parts, as shown.

STEP 5
Use your lining pen to go over the lines that will be visible in the completed drawing and add the finishing touches, including some basic shading, as shown. Erase any pencil lines.

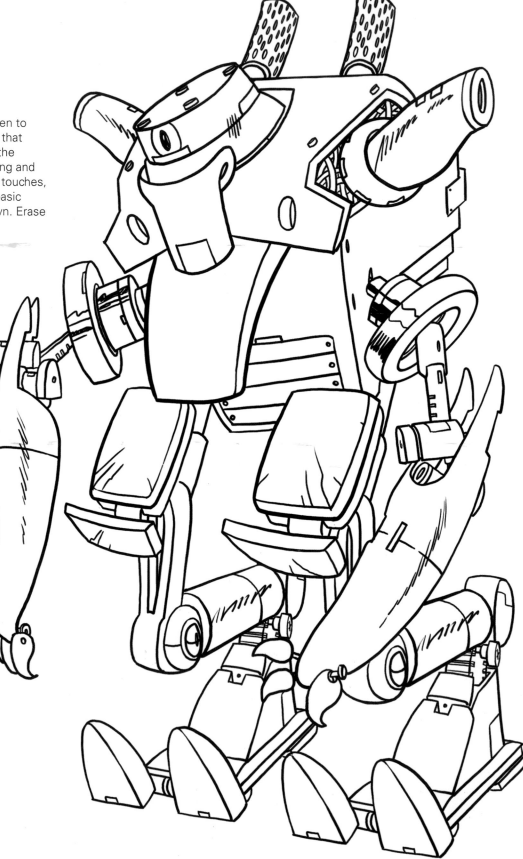

STEP 6

Use brown, rusty base colors to help create the old, battered appearance of this mecha.

ARTIST'S TIP
Dull colors make the mecha appear homemade – lots of bright colors will make it look like an expensive, factory-made machine. Try looking around your home for general household items you can build into your design as well.

STEP 7
Complete the shading using darker colors. Much of the robot is in shadow, which adds to the melancholy feel of the drawing.

WARRIOR MECHA

This mecha has been designed to fill its enemies with fear. The large shoulders make it look powerful and the blades pointing in many directions suggest it is untouchable. We have drawn it from below, so it looks even more intimidating.

STEP 1
Draw a stick figure with his right shoulder angled towards you. His feet are pointed downwards and there are two spikes extending from his hips.

STEP 2
Use rectangular box shapes to give bulk to his arms and legs. Draw the line of his neck and wedge shapes for his hands.

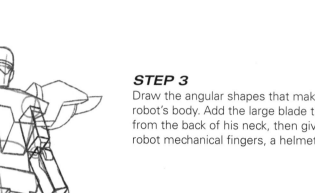

STEP 3

Draw the angular shapes that make up the robot's body. Add the large blade that extends from the back of his neck, then give your robot mechanical fingers, a helmet, and eyes.

STEP 4

Put the finishing touches to your robot by drawing blades extending from his shoulders, upper arms, and hips. Add details to his helmet and body, as shown.

STEP 5
Use your lining pen to go over the lines that will be visible in the finished drawing and add the details to the robot's knees. Erase any pencil lines.

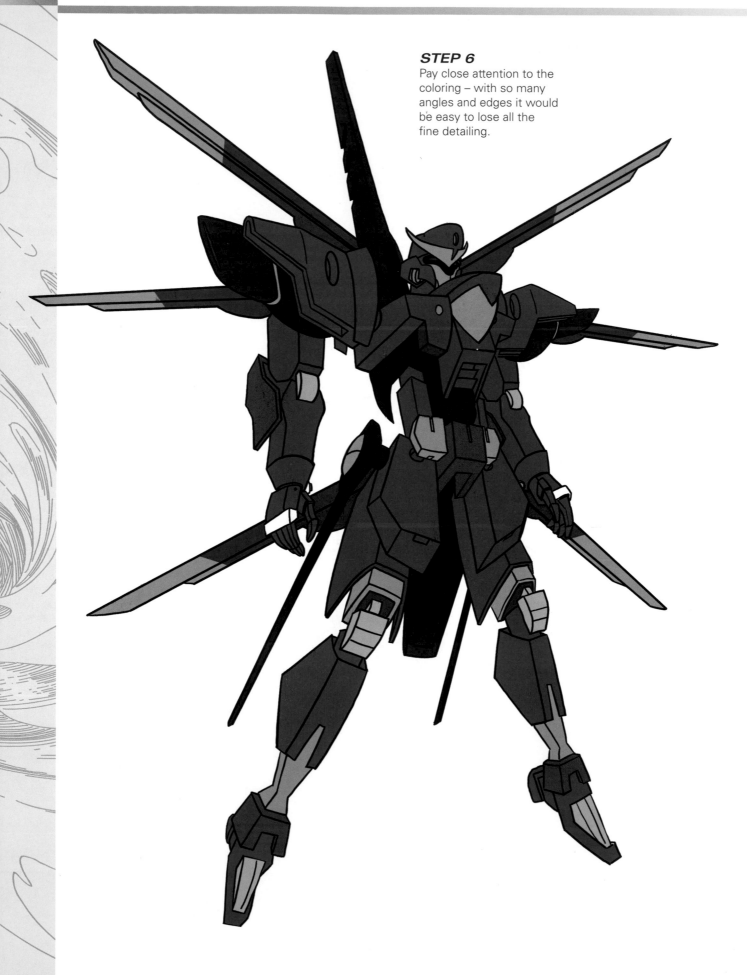

STEP 6
Pay close attention to the coloring – with so many angles and edges it would be easy to lose all the fine detailing.

STEP 7

When adding shading and highlights, it is important to avoid making too many dark shadows. This will preserve the fine edges of your mecha.

DRAWING MECHA

Grinding gears, hot oil, the clank of metal, and the whine of hydraulics can only mean a huge mecha is approaching. Mecha machines can be some of the most fun creations to draw and they allow you to really let your imagination run wild. If you keep a few simple techniques in mind, you can create mecha that will leave all who see them in awe.

Bigger is better

Playing with the scale of surrounding elements can be key to drawing outstanding mecha. A simple way to make your mecha massive is draw the background elements smaller.

Adding a set of power lines and shadows that are edged with leaf shapes has massively increased the apparent scale of this mecha.

You can place your mecha in a city quite easily by drawing scaled-down building silhouettes. Notice how the bridge in the background also increases the scale.

Rust and oil rocks

Adding some wear and tear to your creation will make it look more battle-hardened and believable. Of course, there is a place for pristine mecha when they first roll off the production line, but one that looks as if it's seen a bit of action is much more fun to draw.

Rust can be added to your mecha by creating patches like these on the main metalwork. You can lightly shade them to create the right look.

Damage from scrapes and bangs is easy to add with some simple dark crosshatch shading. Add some slightly thicker lines among the shading to indicate a more serious dent.

Oil leaking from your mecha's hinges shows it has had a rough time. It should be colored in black with important white highlights along the drip. Oil leaks indicate that this mecha is in need of attention if its vital fluids are not to drip away.

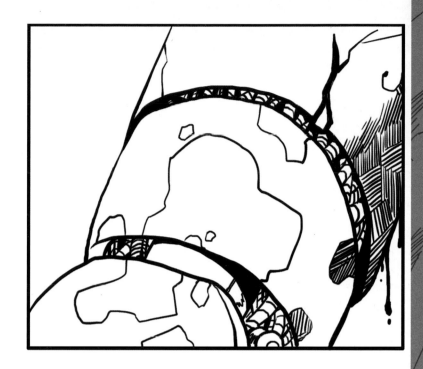

Try a new view

To give your mecha massive scale without taking up the whole page, adjust your viewpoint. Instead of a standard straight-on pose, try drawing the mecha from below.

Using foreshortening to make the upper body parts smaller will create height. Thicker lines for your inking as you get lower down the body will also help greatly with this sense of scale and weight.

CITY MECHA

Your mecha does not have to be based on a human body shape. In the cities of the future, robots can carry out all sorts of tasks. What job do you think this mecha was created for? Does it follow its programming or is it starting to think for itself?

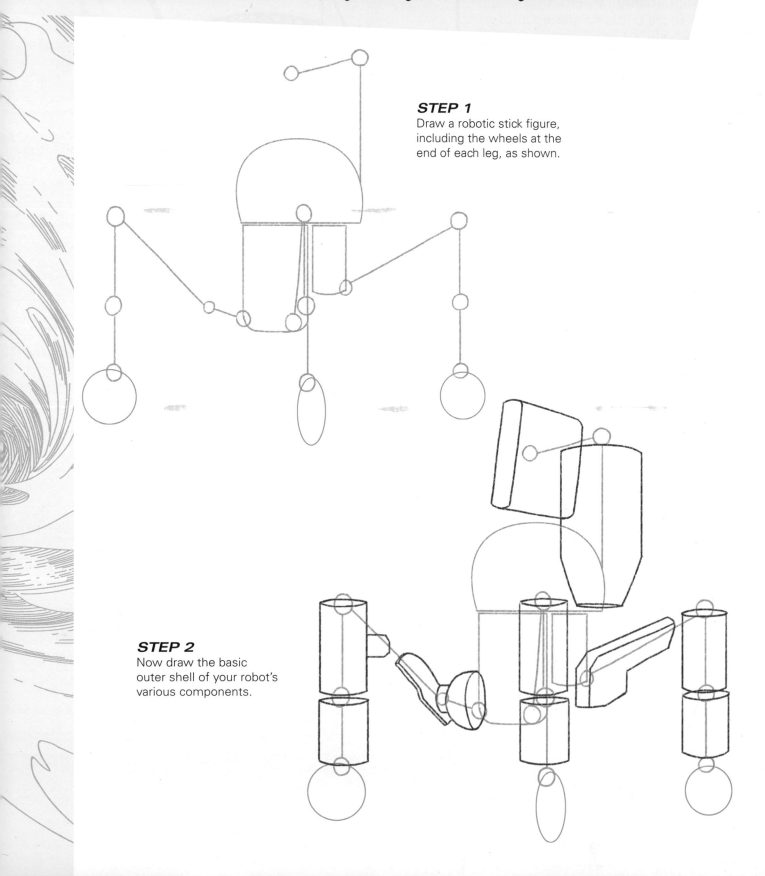

STEP 1
Draw a robotic stick figure, including the wheels at the end of each leg, as shown.

STEP 2
Now draw the basic outer shell of your robot's various components.

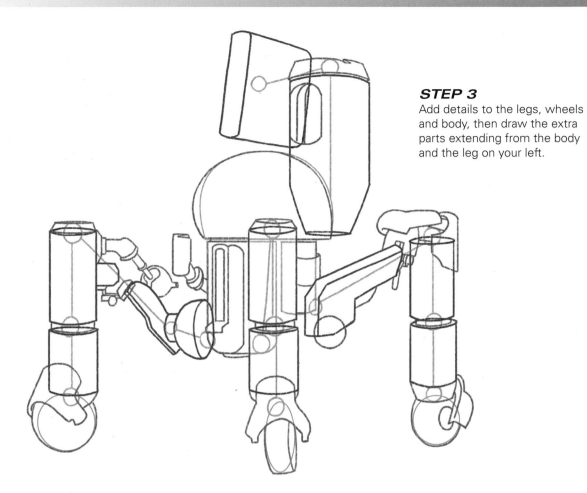

STEP 3

Add details to the legs, wheels and body, then draw the extra parts extending from the body and the leg on your left.

STEP 4

Now put the finishing touches on your robot's construction details, as shown.

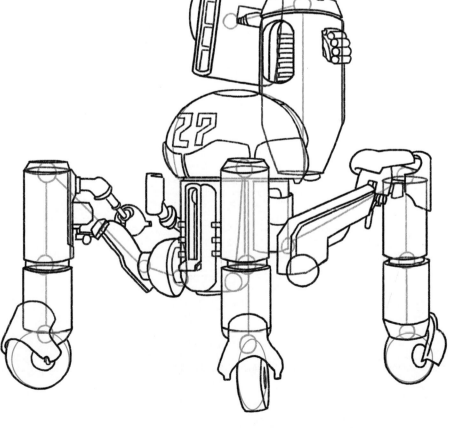

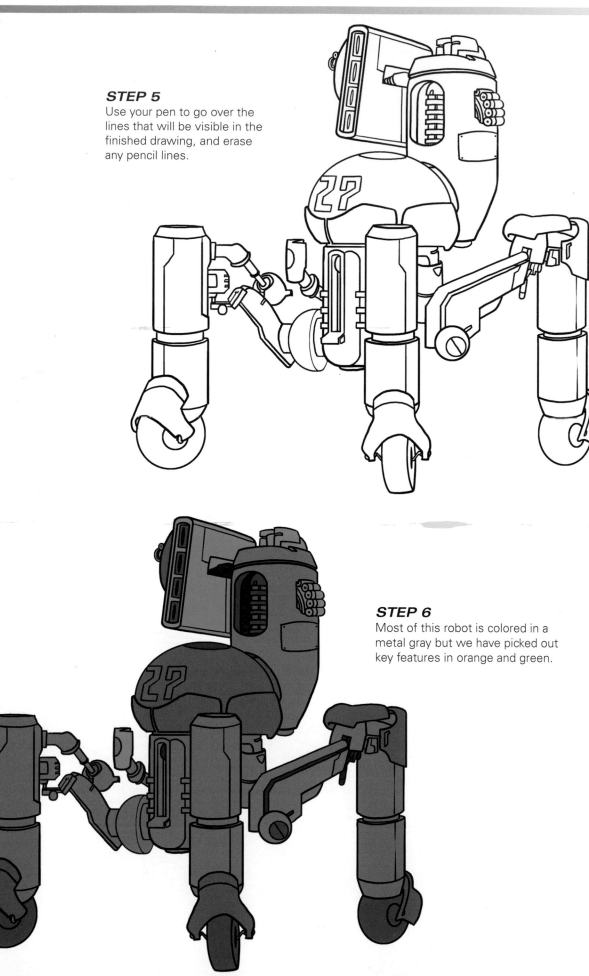

STEP 5
Use your pen to go over the lines that will be visible in the finished drawing, and erase any pencil lines.

STEP 6
Most of this robot is colored in a metal gray but we have picked out key features in orange and green.

ARTIST'S TIP

We have included a number on the dome of this robot. This means the reader can identify our character when it is among other robots of the same type.

STEP 7

Use darker colors to add shading to your drawing. In this case the light is coming from the left-hand side.

MECHA TEAM

The story options are endless with this interesting pair. Was the mecha created to be the boy's bodyguard? Or are they equals, working together to save the world? Perhaps the robot has rescued the boy, and this is the start of their friendship.

STEP 1
You will need to draw two stick figures for this illustration – a giant robot in a crouching position and a boy standing where the robot's right hand will be.

STEP 2
Use cylinder shapes to bulk out the limbs of both figures and draw the lines of their necks. Draw the basic shapes of the hands for the boy and the robot. The robot's right hand is extended beneath the boy with the palm facing upwards.

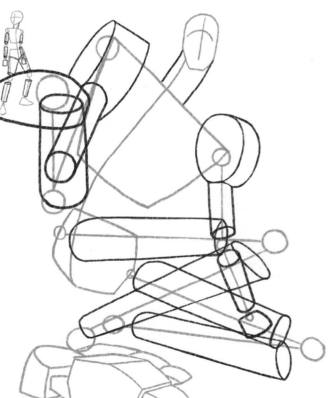

STEP 3
Draw the boy's basic anatomical details and facial features. Draw the fingers of the robot's right hand, cupped around the boy, then add more detail to the robot's face and body, as shown.

STEP 4
Give the boy some clothes, hair and a baseball cap. Add large blades to the robot's shoulders and more detail to his face and body parts.

STEP 5

Use your lining pen to go over the lines that will be visible in the completed drawing. Add pockets to the boy's shirt and put the finishing touches to the robot. Erase any pencil lines.

STEP 6

Different tones of red have been used for the base colors. These help to define the different parts of the mecha, while keeping a single color scheme.

ARTIST'S TIP

Even though you won't see it on the final image, it's important to know how the furthest arm is positioned. Understanding the way the robot is balanced will help you get the pose right.

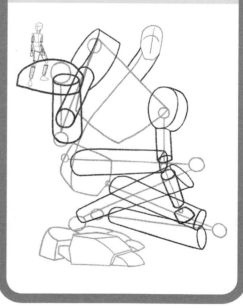

STEP 7
Use darker color to add shading. The light source is on your left, throwing a shadow of the robot's head onto the blade extending from his left shoulder.

BETTER BACKGROUNDS

Your backgrounds will set the mood for your stories and make your world believable. You can think of your backgrounds as another character in your story, so take care getting them right. Always be specific in what you portray and make it appropriate to the setting.

Detail is key
A battered garbage can might fit your storyline better than a pristine one.

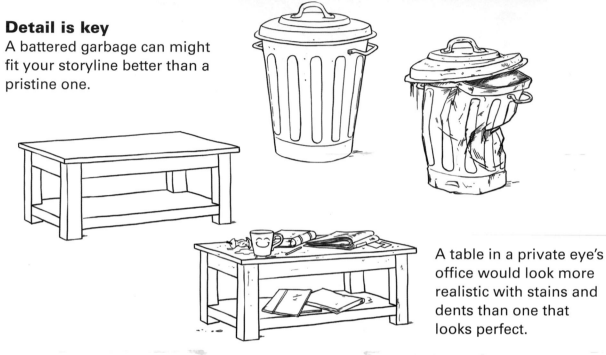

A table in a private eye's office would look more realistic with stains and dents than one that looks perfect.

Everything matters
Look at these two pictures of a seedy city backstreet. Which one do you think you'd find a dangerous gang member hanging out in?

What's over there?
Try not to limit your backgrounds to what is immediately apparent. Use the distant background area to hint at something more going on beyond what you can see.

Backgrounds don't have to be detailed. Here, a shadowy shape is enough to make this forest seem vast.

This road leads to other areas out of the reader's view.

The different tones suggest the city stretches far into the distance.

Less can be more
There's no need to include a fully drawn background on every panel. It is enough to include one per page to let your reader know where the scenes are set. You can include selected items from the background in your close-ups, which will tie the panels into one scene.

GIANT SAMURAI

A samurai was a respected warrior in feudal Japan. Here we have taken a bit of history and mixed it with some futuristic technology to create this monster of a machine. Our mecha is feared by his enemies and loyal to his lord, just like a real samurai.

STEP 1

Draw a large stick figure with huge feet and a small head. There are two poles extending from his shoulders.

STEP 2

Use cylinder shapes to give bulk to his arms, legs and the two poles. Note that the lower parts of his arms and legs are far larger than the upper parts. Draw in the lines of his neck and the basic shapes for his hands.

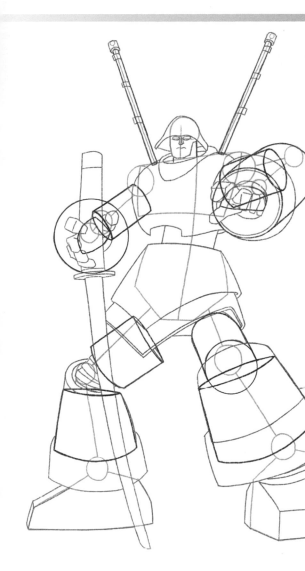

STEP 3
Draw the facial features and fingers, then give your robot a helmet, armor and a large sword. Add details to the two poles.

STEP 4
Draw two flags flying from the poles and add horns and a fierce decoration to the robot's helmet. Add details to the mecha's face, armor, and sword, as shown.

ARTIST'S TIP
Notice how perspective has been used to make the mecha seem massive. The dimensions of the character's top half are slightly smaller.

STEP 5
Complete your robot by adding shading around his face and under his chin. Draw Japanese characters on the flags and the shaft of his sword and add the pattern on the sword's hilt. Use your pen to go over the lines that will be visible in the finished drawing, and erase any pencil lines.

STEP 6
This base coloring looks rather flat, but the correct use of shading at the next stage will give this formidable character a cool, metallic sheen.

愛

義

戦争

STEP 7
Different tones have been used for the shadows to add shape to the mecha.

GLOSSARY

battle-hardened Experienced at fighting.

component A part of a machine.

foreshorten To draw something shorter than it really is so that a picture appears to have depth.

futuristic Looking as if it is set in the future.

gears Toothed wheels that work together to control the speed of a machine.

hydraulics Using liquid forced through tubes to make parts of a machine move.

melancholy A feeling of sadness.

panel One drawing in a cartoon strip.

pristine Undamaged, as if it were new.

private eye A detective who can be hired by a member of the public.

programming The instructions that tell a computer what to do.

scale To judge the size of something by comparing it to something else.

seedy Dirty and uncared for.

silhouette The dark shape an object makes against a bright background.

wear-and-tear The damage caused by everyday use.

FURTHER READING

Draw Your Own Manga: All the Basics by Haruno Nagatomo (Kodansha America, Inc, 2014)

Drawing Manga Mecha, Weapons, and Wheels by Anna Southgate and Yishan Li (Rosen Central, 2012)

Manga Now!: How to Draw Action Figures by Keith Sparrow (Search Press Ltd, 2014)

WEBSITES

Due to the changing nature of Internet links, PowerKids Press has developed an online list of websites related to the subject of this book. This site is updated regularly. Please use this link to access the list: **www.powerkidslinks.com/um/mecha**

INDEX